Ocean Magic

Michael Patrick O'Neill
Batfish Books

O'Neill, Michael Patrick
Ocean Magic / Michael Patrick O'Neill
ISBN 978-0-9728653-5-7
Library of Congress Control Number: 2007904079

Printed in China

Batfish Books
PO Box 32909
Palm Beach Gardens, FL 33420-2909
www.batfishbooks.com

Photographer's Website:
www.mpostock.com

BATFISH
BOOKS

10 9 8 7 6 5 4 3 2 1

Crinoid (*Oxycomanthus bennetti*); Fiji Islands

"Who comes there?"

It's just me, going to work. You see, I'm an undersea explorer and spend a lot of time diving the world's oceans and photographing their creatures.

My job is to tell their stories, and believe me, they have many.

Did you know that the earth's largest living organisms call the ocean home? Do you know why tropical fish are so colorful? And did you know that despite all the problems facing the environment, we can rise to the challenge and turn things around, like we did with one special sea turtle?

Ocean Magic, follow-up to my first book, *Fishy Friends*, aims to illustrate the diversity and complexity of the underwater world and gives its residents a voice.

Photographs speak volumes. Those here narrate their lives and demonstrate spectacular adaptations marine creatures have to make to survive in their complex, fluid environment.

I hope you enjoy them and that they arouse in you an interest in nature.

Best Fishes,

Michael Patrick O'Neill

Big-Eye (*Heteropriacanthus cruentatus*) and Cleaner Goby (*Elacatinus nesiotes*); Cocos Island, Costa Rica

How is a coral reef formed?

Anchored to a base of limestone, coral reefs are made up of many types of coral polyps – tiny, tube-shaped animals only millimeters long. They have a mouth encircled by tentacles on one end and a "foot" on the other.

Related to jellyfish and sea anemones, they live exclusively in marine environments, and all told, there are over 700 varieties, the majority occurring in the Indo-Pacific region.

Most that build reefs are stony corals, named for their hard skeletons of calcium carbonate. As the colonies mature, they can look like the branches of a tree, tables, spheres and countless other shapes.

Stony corals in Fakarava, French Polynesia (both)

Countless varieties of fish populate a coral reef, including *clockwise from left:* Reticulated Dascyllus (*Dascyllus reticulatus*); Beqa Lagoon, Fiji; Long Snou Seahorse (*Hippocampus reidi*); Singer Island, FL; and Clownfish (*Amphiprion percula*); Kimbe Bay, Papua New Guinea.

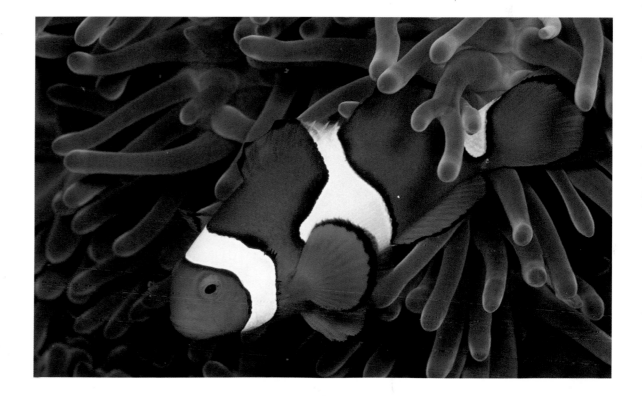

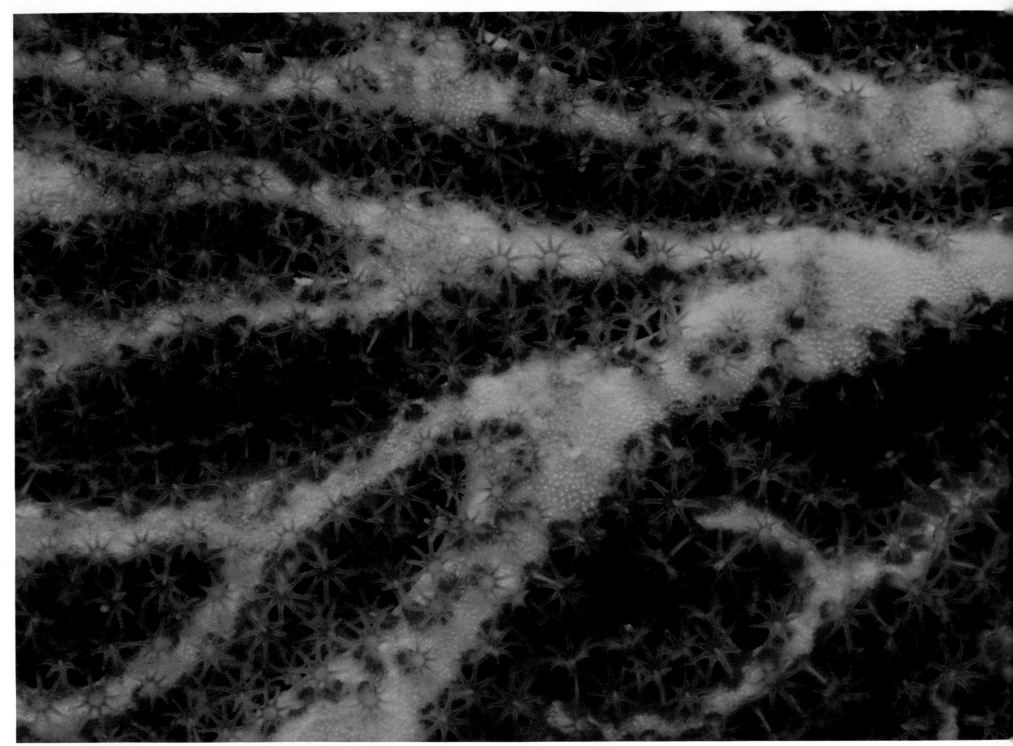

Sea Fan (*Melithaea sp.*); Beqa Lagoon, Fiji Islands (both)

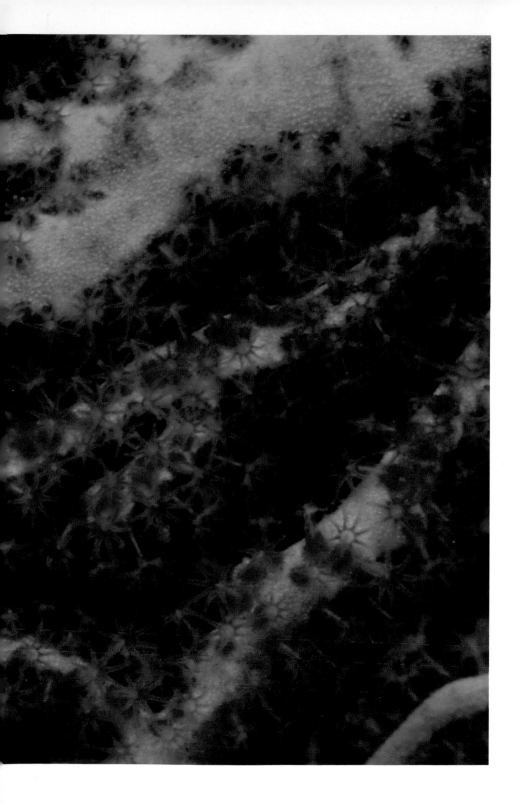

Coral polyps depend on a type of alga called zooxanthella to grow, and since this type of alga needs light to prosper, reefs are usually shallow (less than 300 ft. in depth) and situated in clear seawater.

The water's clarity permits the sun's rays to penetrate the depths and feed the zooxanthellae, which in turn nourish the polyps.

Under ideal conditions, reefs form the largest living organisms on the planet. They are islands of life, oases that attract an unimaginable number of animals.

Soft Coral (*Dendronephthya sp.*)

Since we mentioned algae, let's learn a little bit about kelp, the world's largest variety. While the zooxanthellae are microscopic, kelp is enormous. One type from California can grow two feet per day and reach a length of nearly 150 ft!

A type of brown seaweed that flourishes in colder water, kelp is beneficial to people and animals alike. Kelp-based products are used in items like toothpaste, cooking ingredients and even ice cream. Marine animals living in it use it for both refuge and sustenance.

Diving through a kelp forest is like taking a stroll through an unreal world populated with awesome and bizarre creatures. The Pacific coast of North America and New Zealand contain the most breathtaking kelp forests around.

Let's take a look at some of their inhabitants.

Ecklonia Kelp (*Ecklonia radiata*)

Flapjack (*Carpophyllum maschalocarpum*) and Strap Kelp (*Lessonia variegata*), identified by its thicker blades; Poor Knights Marine Reserve, New Zealand (both)

Jewel Anemones (*Corynactis haddoni*); Poor Knights Marine Reserve, New Zealand

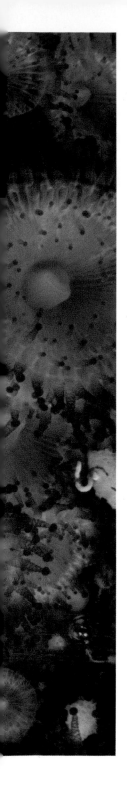

Top: Red Irish Lord
(*Hemilepidotus hemilepidotus*);
Right: Wolf Eel
(*Anarrhichthys ocellatus*);
British Columbia (both)

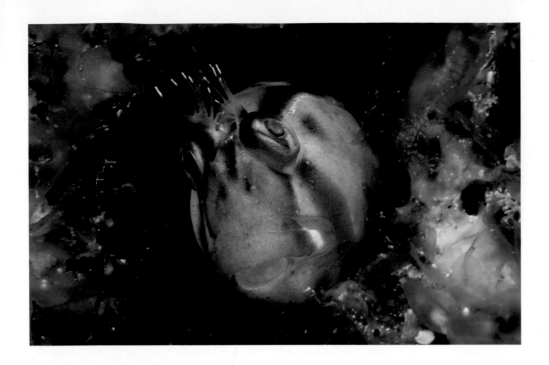

Top: Crested Blenny
(*Parablennius laticlavius*);
Right: Blue Cod
(*Parapercis colias*)

Sea Urchin (*Diadema palmari*); Poor Knights Marine Reserve, New Zealand (all)

Locked with coral in a never-ending war for territory, sponges are among the most simple and primitive of animals.

Found worldwide, including on warm-water reefs and kelp forests, they can grow virtually on anything. Over 5,000 species have been documented, and more are discovered regularly.

While sponges lack many traits we would assume necessary for survival, like muscles and internal organs, they have proven to be wildly successful.

Filter feeders, they can pump water through their bodies to eat and clean themselves. And to make life easier, they grow on places with the strongest currents – exactly where many corals like to live. As you can imagine, they aren't the best neighbors.

Sponges contain toxic chemicals that can harm corals and many predators. This makes them especially interesting to scientists, who believe one day that they may harness the sponges' "chemical warfare" tactics and weapons to fight cancer.

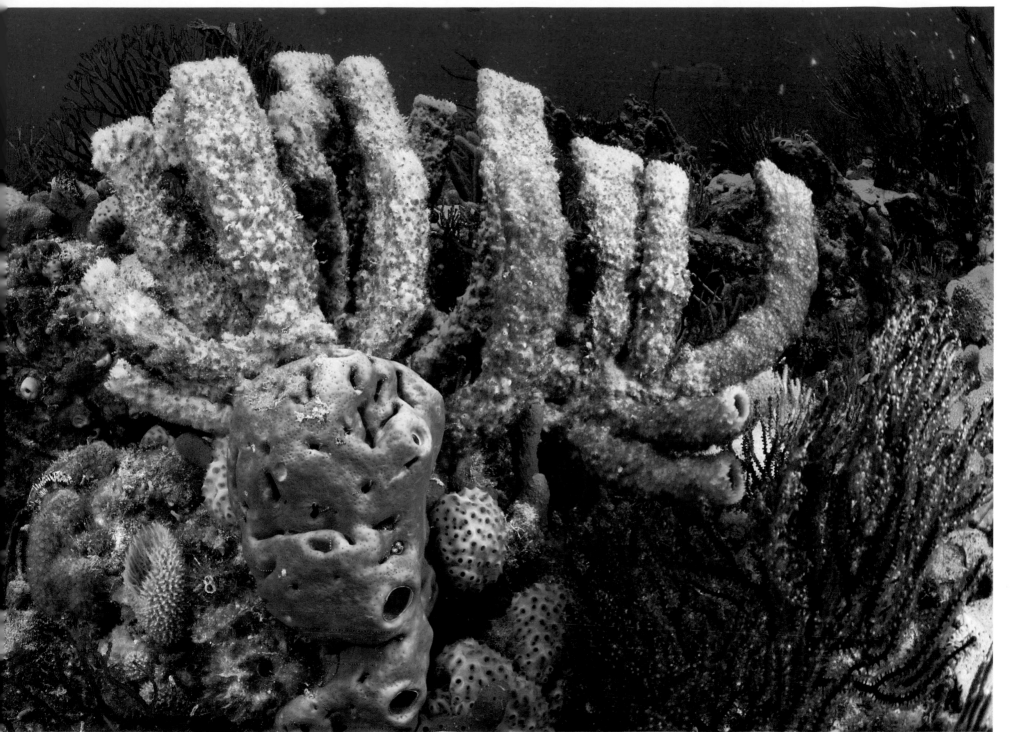

Turf war: several species of sponges and coral fight for space in a Palm Beach, FL reef.

16

Have you ever wondered why reef fish are so colorful?

They use their incredibly flashy colors to court, warn, threaten, fight or hide.

This visual communication based on color is possible because of the crystalline world they live in. It allows them to see and signal each other over great distances – up to 200 ft. in certain locations free from pollution and plankton blooms.

By contrast, fish in murky habitats are far less gaudy. Instead of enjoying unlimited visibility, they're lucky to have just a few inches. And therefore, they rely primarily on touch, taste and smell.

Bannerfish (*Heniochus acuminatus*); Rangiroa, French Polynesia

Spotted Sharpnose Puffer (*Canthigaster punctatissima*); Cocos Island, Costa Rica

Big Eye Trevally (*Caranx sexfasciatus*); Rangiroa, French Polynesia (both)

Every square inch of ocean bottom shelters an animal of some sort. Think of each one as a champion, for it beat almost impossible odds to claim its territory.

Every day is a life and death struggle. The underwater world is brimming with predators that come in all shapes, sizes and disguises.

They never take a day off, and danger is constant.

Hawksbill Turtle (*Eretmochelys imbricata*)

Watching, smelling and feeling, this Sand Tiger (*Carcharias taurus*) is an accomplished hunter of large and medium-sized fish like snapper and grouper. Sharks, with rays and skates, are part of the Elasmobranch family of fish.

Goliaths form large spawning aggregations every fall in Jupiter, FL, and it's the ideal location to see the giants up close.

The Goliath Grouper (*Epinephelus itajara*), another master hunter, delights in inhaling ornamental fish, grunts, small sea turtles and lobster with its gargantuan mouth.

Reaching 7 ft. in length and 800 lbs., the Goliath is found in shipwrecks and caves. Quite appropriately, its species name (*itajara*) means "Lord of the Rocks" in Tupi-Guarani, a native Brazilian language.

Easy pickings for fishermen, this mammoth fish is rare throughout its range, the Atlantic and Eastern Pacific. In Florida, it has made an impressive comeback since receiving protection in 1990.

This species of frogfish grows to about 8 inches. Singer Island, FL (both)

Meet the connoisseur of camouflage, the Striated or Hairy Frogfish (*Antennarius striatus*), a member of the Anglerfish family.

Simply put, this consummate predator is the nightmare of small fish. It practically disappears in the seaweed and "fishes" for prey by shaking a fleshy appendage known as an *esca*, which is connected to its mouth via a thin spine.

If the fishing is poor in one location, the Striated Frogfish will walk clumsily to a new spot and try again. Any fish that gets too close is swallowed in a lightning-fast ambush.

This little monster is another example of how carnivorous fish occupy every single level of the marine food chain.

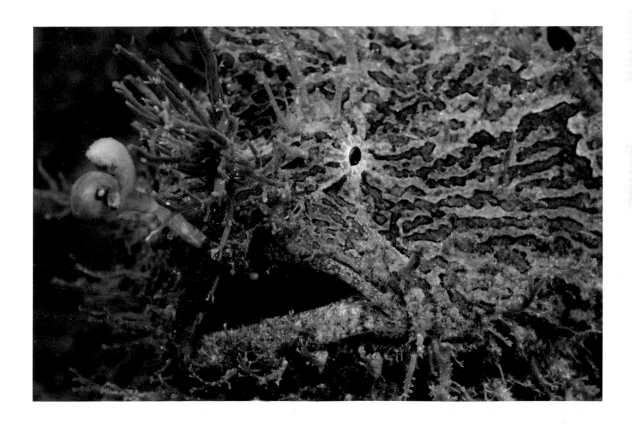

Cousins of snails, nudibranches are among the most colorful and voracious hunters in the ocean. Think of it this way: if sharks were as ravenous as nudibranches, we would *really* be in trouble!

These pint-size predators are meat eaters, and some are even able to use the poison from hydroids, a favorite prey related to jellyfish, to defend themselves.

"Nudibranch" comes from the Latin and Greek words *nudus* and *brankhia*, respectively, which mean *naked gill*. This unusual name is suitable since many varieties have exposed gills on their backs.

Verconis Nudibranch (*Tambja verconis*)

Gem Nudibranch (*Dendrodoris denisoni*); Poor Knights Marine Reserve, New Zealand (both)

Sequence from the Poor Knights
Marine Reserve in New Zealand
showing a pair of nudibranches
(*Ceratosoma amoena*) mating
(left) and a female depositing
eggs (top).

Nudibranches lay their eggs in a
spiral (right). Subject to predation
and currents, most eggs are lost.

We reign supreme over all predators and catch an almost incomprehensible amount of food fish every year from the oceans – 80 million metric tons. This volume is five times the quantity taken 50 years ago due to an overabundance of fishing boats and innovations in technology.

Even reef fish and invertebrates are in demand. Despite progress made in fish farming for aquariums, most specimens are still caught in the wild. The latest reports indicate 20 million reef fish, 10 million invertebrates and 12 million stony corals are collected annually to decorate home tanks.

In reality, nobody owns or controls these resources, and people try to take as much as possible, never thinking about tomorrow before it's too late.

Snook poachers, Singer Island, FL

A tropical fish collector heads to the surface with his catch. Palm Beach, FL

A Kemp's Ridley (*Lepiochelys kempii*) makes an extremely unusual appearance on a deep reef in Palm Beach, FL (both).

While we have the ability to do great harm to the marine environment, we also have the know-how to fix things when they do go wrong. The success story of the Kemp's Ridley demonstrates this superbly and is an inspiration to us all.

The smallest and rarest of all sea turtles, the Kemp's Ridley almost vanished due to egg collecting and drowning in shrimp nets in the Gulf of Mexico, its home range.

Changes in fishing practices and the protection and relocation of nests in Mexico and Texas in the 1980s and 1990s brought it back from the brink of extinction.

In 1985, scientists estimated there were only 500 adult females left. Today, they believe this figure has tripled and are encouraged by the progress made through teamwork and cooperation.

Silvertip (*Carcharhinus albimarginatus*); Rangiroa, French Polynesia

The Ocean Realm
Frequently Asked Questions

One of the most enjoyable aspects of my work is presenting every year to thousands of school children and introducing them to the ocean realm. They always ask many questions about my experiences diving and photographing. Here's a sample of their favorites:

Does the pressure hurt your ears when SCUBA diving?

No. When descending, divers slowly equalize their ears to the water pressure in several ways, among them swallowing or moving their jaws. This way, there is no discomfort.

Is it easy to photograph marine animals?

Some are easy while others are extremely shy and hard to find. The photographer must always be respectful of the animals down there. It's important to move cautiously. As a result, they can become accustomed to your presence, and the odds of taking a great picture increase dramatically.

Where is your favorite place to dive?

French Polynesia. These remote islands in the Pacific have the clearest, bluest water in the world and a rich assortment of wildlife, particularly sharks.

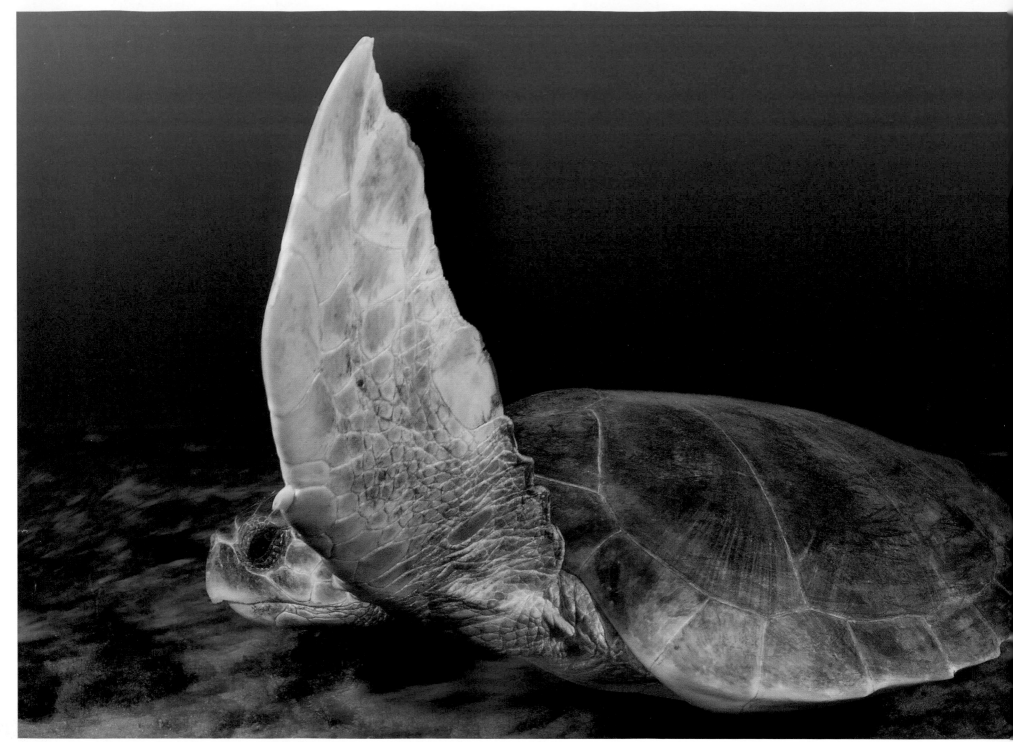

Loggerhead Sea Turtles (*Caretta caretta*); Juno Beach, FL (left) and Palm Beach, FL

How can we help save the oceans?

The little things we do all add up, especially picking up trash. Recently, I came across this specific Loggerhead (left). Entangled in fishing line, she would have drowned if I didn't cut her loose. Every time I dive, I remove as much line as possible to prevent a turtle from drowning. If that helps, then I'm doing my part.

What happens to marine animals when they die?

Scavengers such as sharks, crabs, starfish and worms quickly eat animals that die on the reef. That's why it's so important to protect these "garbage collectors," so they can continue keeping the oceans clean and healthy.

Are stingrays dangerous?

No. Stingrays are calm animals that spend most of the time resting on the bottom. Since they have a sharp spine on the tail, it pays to be careful when wading in murky water to reduce the risk of stepping on one by mistake. By the way, they can get huge, reaching 7 ft. across and weighing more than 600 lbs.

How about moray eels?

People bitten by morays are either putting their hands into holes looking for lobster or feeding the snake-like fish. The chances of it happening are close to zero. This Mosaic Moray (*Enchelycore ramosa*) from New Zealand is actually very shy. It uses its toothy grin to intimidate predators.

Roughtail Stingray (*Dasyatis centroura*); Jupiter, FL

Bottlenose Dolphins (*Tursiops truncatus*)

Final Thoughts

Wild dolphins, especially Bottlenose, don't usually stay around scuba divers. After all, we're loud, clumsy and don't move fast enough to entertain them. These, in Rangiroa, French Polynesia, were the exception. They hung around for minutes, imitating our swimming movements.

Wild animals most often run away from us. So when they approached, it was cause for celebration. For a moment, it seemed like time stood still, and we bridged a gap between species. Playing with the dolphins became the most important thing we could do during that magical time.

Currents, boat schedules, sharks and life could all wait.

Glossary

Alga
Seaweed
Plural: Algae

Anemone
Bottom-dwelling, tentacle-filled
animal related to corals

Anglerfish
A fish known for using part
of its body as a lure to "fish"
for prey

Calcium Carbonate
Hard, rock-like substance
produced by stony corals

Camouflage
The ability of an animal to hide
using its shape or color

Coral Polyp
Small tube-shaped animal with
a mouth on one end and a "foot"
on another

Elasmobranch
Family of fish that includes
sharks, rays and skates

Esca
A worm-like limb used by anglerfish
to attract prey

Filter Feeder
An animal that strains food from
the water like a sponge

Indo-Pacific
Region covering the west coast
of the Americas to eastern Africa

Kelp
Type of seaweed found in seawater
not warmer than 70° Fahrenheit

Strawberry Anemones (*Corynactis californica*); British Columbia, Canada

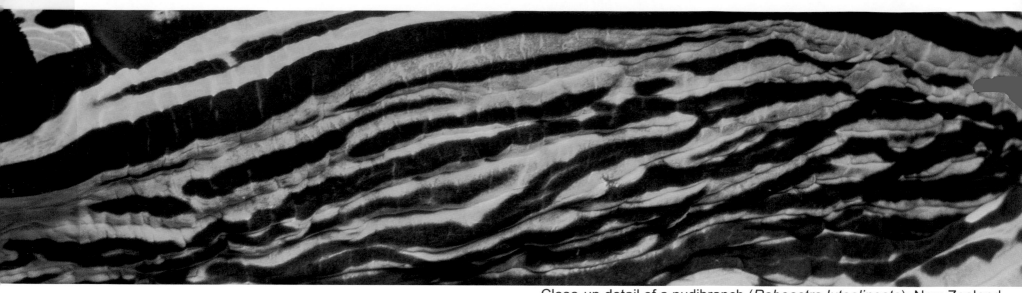

Close-up detail of a nudibranch (*Roboastra luteolineata*); New Zealand

Limestone
Rock comprised of calcium carbonate

Metric Ton
Approximately 2,204 lbs.

Nudibranch
Marine slug related to land snails

SCUBA
Equipment used for diving; acronym for Self Contained Underwater Breathing Apparatus

Soft Coral
Coral that does not form calcium carbonate

Spawning Aggregation
Gathering of fish at a specific time to lay eggs

Sponge
Primitive animal that absorbs food from the water

Stony Coral
Coral that forms calcium carbonate

Temperate Habitat
Region that experiences non-polar, non-tropical weather and sea conditions

Tupi-Guarani
Native Brazilian dialect and source of the Goliath Grouper's species name in Latin

Zooxanthella
A tiny alga found inside coral polyps
Plural: Zooxanthellae

Batfish Books - Your Passport to Learning & Exploration!

ISBN 978-0-9728653-1-9
$15.95

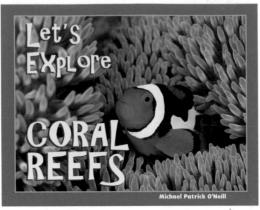

ISBN 0-9728653-3-0
$15.95

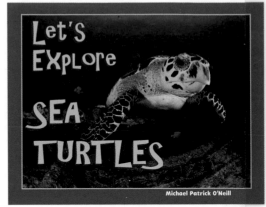

ISBN 0-9728653-2-2
$15.95

ISBN 978-0-9728653-5-7
$19.95

ISBN 978-0-9728653-4-0
$19.95

ISBN 0-9728653-0-6
$19.95

Batfish Books   P.O. Box 32909   Palm Beach Gardens, FL   33420

info@batfishbooks.com   www.batfishbooks.com